Also available from Lowell House and
Lowell House Juvenile:

The Official Freebies® for Fans
The Official Freebies® for Kids

The Official

for Teachers
New Edition

By the Editors of *Freebies* **Magazine**

Illustrations by Leo Abbett

Lowell House
Los Angeles

CONTEMPORARY BOOKS
Chicago

Copyright © 1995 by Freebies Publishing Company.
All rights reserved. No part of this work may be reproduced or transmitted in any form or by any means, electronic or mechanical, including photocopying and recording, or by any information storage or retrieval system, except as may be expressly permitted by the 1976 Copyright Act or in writing by the publisher.

ISBN 1-56565-234-7

Requests for such permissions should be addressed to:

Lowell House
2029 Century Park East, Suite 3290
Los Angeles, CA 90067

Publisher: Jack Artenstein
Director of Publishing Services: Rena Copperman
Original Text Design: Brenda Leach/Once Upon a Design

Manufactured in the United States of America

10 9 8 7 6 5 4 3 2 1

Why Freebies??

"Why do they give it away?" Marketers, from companies large and small, are looking to win the battle for your dollars, and product sampling is an effective way to attract attention and make a positive impression. Studies show that allowing you to sample a company's product is more likely to result in a purchase than other marketing campaigns.

About This Book

Freebies for Teachers contains more than 150 freebie offers that are sure to appeal to teachers and students alike, but you don't have to be a teacher to order from this book. Each offer has been described as accurately as possible to help you decide which offers are best for you.

Unlike offers in other "get things free" books, we have confirmed that each supplier wants you to have the offers listed in this book, and each supplier has agreed to have adequate stock on hand to honor all properly made requests. Many suppliers will make quantity discounts available. If you see something you like, write and ask about quantity discounts.

Some teachers have written and told us that they use the offers to set up a writing lesson. Students look through *Freebies for Teachers* and select an offer. The letter writing encourages good penmanship and spelling and the proper way to write a business-type letter.

How to Use Freebies for Teachers

1. *Follow the directions:* Each offer specifies how to order the freebie. Some offers may ask for a long SASE (a long self-addressed, stamped envelope with the requested postage). Be sure to check the amount of postage requested. Some offers will require two first-class stamps. Likewise, offers from Canada will require the correct postage amount. Since postal rates are changing, check with your local Post Office to determine the correct first-class postage to Canada. If a small postage and handling fee is requested (P&H), include the proper amount (a check or money order is usually preferred). Some suppliers may wait for out-of-town checks to clear before honoring requests. Use a single piece of tape to affix any coins.

2. *Print all information:* Not everyone's handwriting is easy to read. It is safer to print your name, address, and the complete spelling of your city and state on your request. Be sure to include your return address on the outside of your mailing envelope. Use a ballpoint pen, typewriter, or computer to make your requests. Pencils can often smear, and felt-tip or ink pens smudge easily.

3. *Allow time for your request to be processed and sent:* Some suppliers send their offers via first-class mail. Others use bulk-rate mail, which can take up to eight weeks. Suppliers get thousands of requests each year and may process them slowly or right away, depending on the time of year.

4. *What to do if you are unhappy with your freebie product:* If you are unhappy or have complaints about an offer, or if you have not received an offer within eight to ten weeks of your request, let *FREEBIES* know. Although the *FREEBIES* editors do not stock items or offer refunds from their offices, they can follow up on your complaints with any supplier. Occasionally there are problems with a particular supplier or offer and your letters help to alert us. Suppliers that generate too many complaints will not be included in future editions. Send your complaints, comments, or suggestions to:

> FREEBIES Book Editors
> 1135 Eugenia Place
> P.O. Box 5025
> Carpinteria, CA 93014-5025

5. *And there is more!* If you like the freebie offers in this book and want to see more free offers, then you should subscribe to *FREEBIES* Magazine. Five times a year, *FREEBIES* sends you a great magazine with approximately 100 current freebie offers in each issue. Purchasers of *Freebies for Teachers* can get a special price on a one-year/five-issue subscription of only $4.95. (The regular subscription rate is $8.95—you'll save $4.00. See the special offer on page 79.)

Acknowledgments

It is difficult to put together a book of this nature without the help of talented and dedicated people working together. The staff at *FREEBIES* has a special thanks for the commitment of RGA/Lowell House to this project. Their support made it happen.

Special mention must be given to Chris Hemesath, Brenda Pope-Ostrow, Rena Copperman, Lisa-Theresa Lenthall, Laurie Young, and the rest of the crew at RGA/Lowell House for the editing, the design, and the final push to complete the project.

Thank-yous are also reserved for Linda Cook and Abel Magaña for their help and guidance. A special thanks to Don Weiner for the research, writing, and editing of the material in this book.

Flu Tips

GET-WELL CARD

☆ Few things can disrupt the classroom worse than the annual outbreak of influenza and stomach flu. Help educate your students to key preventive measures with this **free flu information card** from the makers of Imodium A-D. Each 4" x 9" chart outlines the causes and symptoms of flu, plus offers relief tips for both intestinal and respiratory flu.

Send: Your name & address

Ask For: Imodium A-D Flu Tips

Mail To: Imodium A-D
1675 Broadway, 33rd Fl.
Drawer F
New York, NY 10019

Water Brochure

THE BEST BEVERAGE

☆ The average body is made up of 55 to 75% water, yet many of us overlook its importance in the average diet. This **free 10-page brochure, *"Water: The Beverage for Life"*** pours over the basics, including when we need water the most, how it helps athletic performance, and an overview of federal safety regulations for both bottled and tap water.

Send: A long SASE

Ask For: Water: The Beverage for Life

Mail To: Water: The Beverage for Life
International Bottled Water Assn.
113 North Henry St.
Alexandria, VA 22314

Science Project Plan

THE MAD SCIENTIST

☆ Even Dr. Frankenstein couldn't always think of a new science project every year. But the Mad Scientist can, and he will send you **one free sample science project plan** and a listing of over 200 more science project plans that are available. Your sample plan will include a list of all needed materials, instructions, and a drawing of what the project should look like upon completion. The Mad Scientist has lots of ideas and wants to share one with you.

Send: A name/address label and two first-class stamps

Ask For: One Sample Science Project Plan

Mail To: The Mad Scientist
Science South
P.O. Box 124
Elkmont, AL 35620

Rubber Stamps

STAMP OUT FUN

☆ Grading papers is often a tough task for teachers, but it can be fun with a **teacher's stamp**. You'll receive one rubber stamp mounted on a 1" wooden block selected from nine designs, all with an educational theme such as a reward ribbon, a school bus, or an "apple from teacher." Also included are 10 mini-stickers, a catalog, and a coupon.

Send: $1.75 P&H for one stamp; $1.25 for each additional stamp

Ask For: Teacher Stamp and Stickers

Mail To: Something for Everyone
P.O. Box 711
Woodland Hills, CA 91365

Totline Newsletter

LINE UP THE KIDS

☆ If you're at a loss for entertaining the youngsters, pick up **a sample copy of *Totline*.** Helpful for teachers, this 32-page bimonthly newsletter will provide you with the perfect guide to keep young children happily active. It's filled with original and easy-to-implement ideas and is perfect for kids in preschool and kindergarten. Included are songs, games, and story ideas.

Send: $1.00 P&H

Ask For: Sample of *Totline Newsletter*

Mail To: Warren Publishing House, Inc.
P.O. Box 2250
Everett, WA 98203

Personalized Postcards

PRETTY AS A PICTURE

☆ Here's a great class project for a great price. You can have your students bring in photos of their families or favorite trips and make up **Personalized Picture Postcards.** Order a pack of 6 or a pack of 100 so all your students can make up several by simply affixing the photos to the adhesive backings. Each card has a pop-out easel for desktop display, and there's plenty of space on the back to write messages and addresses. Cards are available in 3½" x 5" or 4" x 6" size.

Send: $1.50 P&H for six
$6.00 for a pack of 100

Ask For: Personalized Picture Postcard Pack
Indicate quantity and photo size

Mail To: Personalized Picture Postcard
P.O. Box 131
Buffalo, NY 14223-0131

FREEBIES FOR TEACHERS

Sweepstakes Newsletter
GET LUCKY

☆ When you're trying to get by on a teacher's salary, every bit helps. Thousands of lucky people win huge sums of cash and big prizes through corporate-sponsored sweepstakes. Find out how to become one of them by getting a free sample issue of **Best Sweepstakes Newsletter.** Every month this 10-page newsletter publishes approximately thirty listings of current contests.

Send: A long SASE with two first-class stamps
Ask For: Sweepstakes Newsletter Sample
Mail To: Sweepstakes Newsletter
4215 Winnetka Ave. N., Ste. 219
New Hope, MN 55428

Recipe Bookmark
LITE READING

☆ If you want to eat healthy, learn how to cook healthy. Lesson one starts with a **free recipe bookmark.** Each bookmark features a low-fat, low-sugar, low-salt recipe from Kathy Kochan's "De-lite-ful Appetizers" book. You'll also receive information on her other book, "De-lite-ful Desserts."

Send: A long SASE
Ask For: De-lite-ful Bookmark
Mail To: De-lite-ful Books
15 E. Main St.
Mendham, NJ 07945

Sample Newsletter

PENNY WISE

☆ Times are tight and so is your budget. You can learn all the tricks to stretching those dollars with a **sample copy of The Penny Pincher,** a nationally reviewed newsletter that has been referred to as the poor man's **Money** magazine. Typical issues are eight pages, covering everything from cheap travel to home-based businesses.

Send: $1.00 plus a long SASE with one first-class stamp

Ask For: Sample Issue of *The Penny Pincher*

Mail To: The Penny Pincher
P.O. Box 809
Kings Park, NY 11754

Fresh Carrots Brochure

WHAT'S UP DOC?

☆ If you teach your students about nutrition, you already know that carrots should be a big part of their diets. This **free "California Fresh Carrots"** brochure will help you explain why. It covers the benefits of vitamin A, beta carotene, and other nutrients that are found in carrots. You also get some handy recipes to try.

Send: A long SASE

Ask For: California Fresh Carrots Brochure

Mail To: California Carrot Advisory Board
15 Willow St.
Salinas, CA 93901

FREEBIES FOR TEACHERS **13**

World Map
WORLD ON A WALL

☆ This full-color poster won't just brighten your classroom, it will brighten your students by teaching them valuable geographical facts. It's a 21" x 32" **world map poster** from George F. Cram Company, makers of some of the world's finest maps since 1867. In fact, each map has been updated to show all the changes throughout Eastern Europe and the former USSR.

Send: $1.49 P&H

Ask For: World Map Poster CD-8-PST

Mail To: George F. Cram Co.
P.O. Box 426
Indianapolis, IN 46206

Fishing Lure
GREAT CATCH

☆ When you catch a break from class on weekends or during summer vacation, you might enjoy the relaxing sport of fishing. Try the **Jambalaya Cajun Fishing Lure Pack** to help increase your catch. It comes from the great state of Louisiana, known as the "Sportsman's Paradise." You'll receive three different lures from a collection that includes proven winners.

Send: $2.00 P&H

Ask For: Jambalaya Lures Pack

Mail To: Ol' John's Lures
7979 Hwy 3015
Keatchie, LA 71046

Auto Tips
CAR CARE

☆ When it comes to car care, do you feel confused? Even if you're an expert, you'll learn some important things about keeping your automobile in tip-top shape with the **free Car Tips from Firestone.** This 15-page brochure, written by professional racer and certified auto mechanic Pat Lazzaro, contains plenty of valuable information to help you keep your car out of the shop and on the road.

Phone: 1-800-9-FIRESTONE

Ask For: Car Care Tips

Allergy Brochure
NOTHING TO SNEEZE AT

☆ When allergy season hits, everyone wants answers. That includes you and your students. Order one or all of these **three free brochures: "Allergies Are Enough to Make You Sick"** is a basic primer on the symptoms and treatments for allergies; **"Venom Attack Force"** deals with insect sting; and **"How to Make People with Allergies Feel Miserable"** is a lighthearted look at allergy sufferers.

Send: Your name and address

Ask For: Allergy Brochure(s) (specify which ones you want)

Mail To: Allergy Brochure Write Away Offer
Miles Inc.
P.O. Box 3145
Spokane, WA 99220-3145

Contact Lenses
USE YOUR CONTACTS

☆ For those people who don't mind wearing glasses but would prefer to use contact lenses on occasion, now there's an option. Call today for a **certificate for a free trial pair of Bausch & Lomb Occasions single-use disposable contact lenses.** Occasions are designed specifically to complement glasses, not replace them. (Eye-care professional's fees for eye exam and lens fitting are not included.)

Phone: 1-800-494-5454

Ask For: Free Trial Lens Certificate

Construction Tips
REDWOOD PROJECTS

☆ The California Redwood Association would like to give you the green light to start a couple of wood projects in your shop class. They are offering a pair of **free Redwood Construction Tips brochures,** providing complete plans for building a 4' x 4' planter box and a butcher block bench. These are straightforward projects that most novices can complete with ease.

Send: A long SASE

Ask For: Redwood Construction Tips for 4' x 4' Planter and Butcher Block Bench

Mail To: California Redwood Association
Dept. Freebie
405 Enfrente Dr., Ste. 200
Novato, CA 94949

Aluminum Recycling Tips

DO THE CAN-CAN

☆ Get your class involved in aluminum can recycling. Schools can now get **free, "The Great Aluminum Can Roundup" kit.** It contains fun facts, stickers, a poster, a chart, and contest information. The goal of the Great Aluminum Can Roundup is to involve more people in aluminum can recycling. When you send for your free kit, indicate the grade level you teach, and you'll receive appropriate lesson plans.

Send: Your name & address

Ask For: Tips for Schools—The Great Aluminum Roundup

Mail To: Can Manufacturers Institute
1625 Massachusetts Ave. NW
Washington, D.C. 20036

Paste Paper Kit

MARBLE-OUS WORKS OF ART

☆ Chandler Designs, experts in the art of French paper marbling and paste paper, are offering **an introductory paste paper kit** so you and your students can create beautiful, swirling color designs using materials you probably already have in your classroom. You will receive complete instructions and information on the process of French paper marbling.

Send: $1.50 P&H

Ask For: Paste Paper Kit

Mail To: Chandler Designs, Ltd.
9017 Mendenhall Ct., Ste. A
Columbia, MD 21045

Eco-Spout

ONE WORLD, ONE SPOUT

☆ Don't just spout off about the environment—do something about it. **Eco-Spout** provides an easy way to be Earth-friendly by reusing the plastic containers from various products that you usually toss out when empty. The Eco-Spout package includes a universal adapter that fits onto containers like the ones for milk, soft drinks, and detergents.

Send:	$2.00 P&H
Ask For:	Eco-Spout
Mail To:	Jaye Products, Inc. Dept. 6 P.O. Box 10726 Naples, FL 33962

Publications Catalog

STUDY THIS

☆ The California Department of Education offers nearly 400 publications on a wide range of subjects available at low cost to teachers. Whether you need to brush up on history, current affairs, or any other areas of study, you'll want to order this **free catalog** and see what's available.

Send:	Your name & address
Ask For:	Catalog of Publications
Mail To:	Calif. Dept. of Education Catalog of Publications P.O. Box 271 Sacramento, CA 95012-0271

Spendless Newsletter

MORE OF LESS

☆ If the '80s were noted for excess, the '90s will surely be defined by a theme of frugality. Take, for instance, this offer for **two free sample issues of *The Spendless Newsletter*.** This new eight-page publication is the latest to offer suggestions for living well with less expense. Every issue emphasizes crafts and recipes that can be made on a small budget.

Send: Two first-class postage stamps

Ask For: Two Copies of *The Spendless Newsletter*

Mail To: The Spendless Newsletter
P.O. Box 1104
Dingmans Ferry, PA 18328

Healthy Eating Brochure

GOOD NUTRITION

☆ Teaching your students about proper eating habits can be extremely frustrating. You tell them to eat vegetables, and they are more interested in candy bars. The makers of Flintstone vitamins have put together a free booklet entitled **"Broccoli or Brownies? Building Healthy Eating Behaviors in Your Child."** It will provide you with the information you need to make a strong case for good nutrition.

Send: Your name & address

Ask For: Broccoli or Brownies Brochure

Mail To: Broccoli or Brownies
c/o Flintstones Vitamins
303 E. Wacker Dr., Ste. 440
Chicago, IL 60601

Safety Tips

BETTER SAFE THAN SORRY

☆ Safety prevention is important both on the road and at home. Help your students teach their parents and grandparents some important safety lessons they may have forgotten over the years. **"Keep It Safe"** is filled with facts and tips for older Americans on everything from dealing with impaired vision to being extra careful when on medication—and it's free.

Send: A long SASE

Ask For: Keep It Safe

Mail To: Keep It Safe
P.O. Box 3744, Dept. FRB
Washington, D.C. 20007-0244

Depression Brochure

OUT OF DARKNESS

☆ Teachers often see a side of their students that parents sometimes miss. You notice if a child is always angry, irritable, or continually out of sorts. You're well aware if your students lack energy or enthusiasm. The **free brochure "Is Your Child Depressed?"** answers many of the questions centering on the causes for these behavior patterns.

Send: A long SASE

Ask For: Is Your Child Depressed?

Mail To: Dr. Joel Herskowitz
30 Arch St.
Framingham, MA 01701

Computer Tips

DISK DISCUSSION

☆ The day-to-day routine of working on your computer can lead you to take your data for granted. But, as Fuji Computer Products notes in the latest issue of their **free journal, *F1—Computer Tips & Advice*,** data is your work, so it's important that you protect and manage it well. This four-page mini-newsletter contains tips on how to free up space on your hard drive to help store data more efficiently.

Send: Your name & address

Ask For: F1—Computer Tips & Advice

Mail To: F1
P.O. Box 5128
Bergenfield, NJ 07621

Drinking Water Information

GET THE LEAD OUT

☆ There's a reason why bottled water is so popular, and it's not just because of the fancy commercials. Depending on where you live and work, tap water can contain all types of extra minerals—and not the ones that are good for you. The **free brochure "Is There Lead in Your Drinking Water?"** tells you how to find out and what you can do about it once you discover that your water does contain a little something extra.

Send: A long SASE

Ask For: Is There Lead in Your Drinking Water?

Mail To: Dr. Joel Herskowitz
30 Arch St.
Framingham, MA 01701

FREEBIES FOR TEACHERS **21**

Computer Club

SAVE & LEARN

☆ Fuji Computer Products, the makers of excellent floppy disks, have formed the **Fuji Computer Club.** To join, buy a pack of Fuji disks, mail in the proof of purchase symbol, and order the club's free booklet. Each booklet is packed with PC tips, bonus points redeemable for free merchandise, money-saving coupons, and club membership information.

Send: Proof of purchase from Fuji floppy disks

Ask For: Fuji Computer Club Booklet/Membership Information

Mail To: Fuji Computer Club
P.O. Box 52932
Dept. 2710
Phoenix, AZ 85072-2932

Jury Brochure

TRIAL OFFER

☆ Whether you're teaching history, social studies, or current events, there comes a time when you need to discuss every American's right to a trial by jury. **"The American Jury"** explains the privilege and importance of serving on a jury, describes jury selection procedures, the role jurors play in trials, and the difference between criminal and civil cases. At no cost to you, it's an open-and-shut case.

Send: A long SASE

Ask For: The American Jury

Mail To: The American Jury
P.O. Box 3744
Dept. FRB
Washington, D.C. 20007-0244

Child Safety
TIPS ON TOYS

☆ Anyone who cares about children knows that toy safety is more than just child's play. **"Play It Safe!"** gives details on how many of the 100,000 accidents children have with toys each and every year are actually preventable. You'll find advice on how to determine the safety of a toy and which ones to avoid altogether. You may even want to share this free information with members of the PTA.

Send: A long SASE

Ask For: Play It Safe!

Mail To: Play It Safe!
P.O. Box 3744
Dept. FRB
Washington, D.C. 20007-0244

Harmonica Poster
HOHNER SYSTEM

☆ Are you a harmonica enthusiast or a music fan? If so, you probably have a special appreciation for the harmonica, a simple instrument that has played an important role in everything from rock to country to blues. The Hohner Marine Band harmonica will soon celebrate its 100th anniversary, and you can join the centennial celebration by ordering a **22" x 30"** poster commemorating this famous instrument's introduction into the cultural mainstream.

Send: $2.00 P&H

Ask For: Marine Band Anniversary Poster

Mail To: Hohner, Inc.
P.O. Box 9375, Dept. MB
Richmond, VA 23227

Art Month Ideas
MARCH AGAIN

☆ Youth Art Month is an annual observance each March to emphasize the value of art education for all children and to encourage public support for quality school art programs. Although March may have already come and gone, you can get a free copy of the **Youth Art Month Idea Booklet** and make every day an artistic day in your classroom.

Send: Your name & address
Ask For: Youth Art Month Idea Booklet
Mail To: Council for Art Education, Inc.
100 Boylston St., Ste. 1050
Boston, MA 02116

Comic Strip
LIBRARY HI-JINX

☆ Move over, Conan the Barbarian, here's "ALEX . . . the Librarian." This **free comic strip** was developed by a Michigan librarian, and it's a compendium of laughs. Follow Alex as he pokes fun at the world of work, current events, and personal relationships. It seems as if he always gets entangled in topical situations that appeal to both children and adults.

Send: A long SASE
Ask For: Alex the Librarian Comic
Mail To: Alex Krentzin
4157 Cooper St.
Royal Oak, MI 48073

Hiking Safety Brochure

TAKE A HIKE

☆ We mean this in the nicest way possible. In fact, before you hit the trails with your students, we suggest you read this **free "Hiking Safety" brochure.** General guidelines such as planning a trip, dressing properly, bringing proper equipment, and organizing a hiking group are all covered in this eight-page publication.

Send: A long SASE

Ask For: Hiking Safety Brochure

Mail To: American Hiking Society
P.O. Box 20160
Washington, D.C. 20041-2160

Crafts Safety

SMART ART

☆ The Art and Craft Materials Institute, Inc. (ACMI) is a non-profit association that seeks to create and maintain a positive environment for instructors and students who work with art and craft materials. As a reference source of safety guidelines for art and craft products, ACMI is offering a **free information booklet** that will help those working on art projects do so without taking unnecessary health risks.

Send: Your name & address

Ask For: Safety of Arts & Crafts Booklet

Mail To: Art & Craft Materials Institute
100 Boylston St., Ste. 1050
Boston, MA 02116

Soap Kit

SOW IN THE SOAP

☆ Plant flowers right into hand soap with this **decorative pressed flower soap kit.** The kit gives you what you need to create a pretty Victorian-inspired floral design in a soap bar. You get real pressed flower pieces, ribbon, directions, plus tips on pressing flowers and ideas for future projects.

Send: $1.00 P&H

Ask For: Pressed Flower Soap Kit

Mail To: G.A.L.S. Flowers
21 Entwistle Ave.
Nutley, NJ 07110

Money-Saving Tips

MEET THE SKINFLINTS

☆ It has been featured on the cover of Kiplinger's Personal Finance, the nation's top newspapers, and top television talk shows. Now you can get your own **free copy of the *Skinflint News.*** The eight-page monthly newsletter defines "skinflint" as "a thrifty-minded person who saves money by all means possible." If you fit the bill (and most of us do), order a copy today, and start saving tomorrow.

Send: A long SASE

Ask For: Sample Copy of Skinflint News

Mail To: Skinflint News, Dept. F
P.O. Box 818
Palm Harbor, FL 34682

Leak Detection Information

NOT A DROP

☆ What could become the most serious environmental crisis of the year 2000? Not oil, air pollution, or toxic wastes. If nothing changes, the most serious shortage will occur in the most precious resource of all: pure water. Fight the looming crisis with this **free water conservation brochure.** The 12-panel guide gives a checklist to save water at school and at home.

Send: A long SASE with two first-class stamps

Ask For: Conservation Brochure

Mail To: American Leak Detection
888 Research Dr., Ste. 109
Palm Springs, CA 92262

Needlepoint Card

STITCHED IN TRADITION

☆ With a needle and thread Betsy Ross created our flag and wove into the fabric of our nation a tradition of quality unmatched in the world. It is also with great pride and meticulous work that this **Patriotic Bear needlepoint card** was handcrafted in America. This winner comes with an outside-stitched design in beautifully vibrant yarns of a teddy bear waving a flag against a red-white-and-blue background. An envelope complements this 5" x 7" card.

Send: $1.00 P&H (Payable to V. Safro)

Ask For: HandCrafted Needlepoint Card

Mail To: Classic Cards by Vickie
2307 Blanchard Dr.
Glendale, CA 91208

Simple Green Sample

KEEP IT CLEAN

The Clean Solution

☆ Sometimes the school custodian doesn't get crayon or ink stains cleaned up. You can clean up a variety of stains and other messes with this **free sample packet of Simple Green Cleaner,** an environmentally safe, all-purpose concentrate that is biodegradable. You'll receive a sample pack that makes a quart of cleaning solution. Order an extra for the Teacher's Lounge or your home for an additional quarter.

Send:	A long SASE for one; $0.25 for each additional sample
Ask For:	Simple Green Cleaner Sample Pack
Mail To:	Sav-On Dept. SG P.O. Box 1356 Gwinn, MI 49841

Plastic Imprinter

FOSSIL FUN

☆ When you return those science homework assignments, reach back in time and surprise your students with an imprint of a fossil. These **plastic fossil imprinters** make their mark on paper, clay, or other impressionable items. The fossils can be purchased at museum gift shops, but our supplier will send you one for free. They come in three styles, including a fish, a lizard, and a seahorse.

Send:	A long SASE for one; $0.25 for each additional fossil
Ask For:	Fossil Imprinter
Mail To:	Sav-On Dept. FI P.O. Box 1356 Gwinn, MI 49841

Recipe Booklet
SWEET DEAL

☆ Not everyone is sweet on using sugar in recipes. But, for years, honey was the primary sweetener used throughout the world. You can show your students how to cook some great dishes using honey when you order this 96-page, spiral-bound **honey cookbook.** It's filled with over 100 recipes and lots of full-color photographs.

Send: $2.50 P&H

Ask For: Sweetened With Honey—The Natural Way

Mail To: National Honey Board
Dept. FB
P.O. Box 7760
Marshfield, WI 54449

Endangered Species Stickers
NATURAL SELECTION

☆ As the highest evolved creatures on the planet, we humans must protect our most vulnerable animal friends from harm. You can do your own small part and help your students learn an important lesson with this **set of 20 endangered species stickers.** Each colorful sticker depicts a different animal species that is threatened with extinction. Plus, part of the money you send will be donated to the World Widlife Fund to Help the Animals.

Send: $2.00 P&H

Ask For: Endangered Species Sticker Set

Mail To: Stickers N' Stuff
Dept. FBES
P.O. Box 430
Louisville, CO 80027

Sticker Sampler

THAT DECORATIVE TOUCH

☆ Reward your students for a job well done. Give them out as prizes for classroom games. Use them to designate special efforts on homework assignments. Surely you can come up with a number of other great ways to use this **sampler of 12 stickers** that includes holographic, prism, neon, chrome, and pearlescent stickers.

Send: $1.00 plus a SASE

Ask For: 12 Sample Stickers

Mail To: Stickers N' Stuff
Dept. FBT
P.O. Box 430
Louisville, CO 80027

Health Brochure

ASTHMA RISK

☆ Surprisingly, most fatal and near-fatal asthma attacks can be prevented with proper diagnosis and treatment. AZMC has created these **two free American Asthma Alert questionnaires.** The first Alert will indicate if you should see a doctor to determine if you have asthma. The second Alert will help you determine if you are receiving the proper medical care, understand the disorder, and are living to your fullest potential. A third **free brochure on "Taking The Risk Out of Asthma"** is also available.

Ask For: Asthma Alerts and/ or Taking The Risk Out of Asthma

Call: 1-800-777-4350

Money-Saving Tips

THE LOW DOWN ON THE GOOD LIFE

☆ Learn how to save on your electric bill, cut your costs at the grocery store, trim your household budget, and lower your mortgage. How? **Thrifty Lifestyles** is an eight-page tabloid-sized paper that can share all these secrets. This colorful publication brings together the publishers of some of the country's most popular "money-saving newsletters" to help you get the most out of any budget.

Send: $2.00 P&H

Ask For: *Thrifty Lifestyles*

Mail To: Lilac Publishing
P.O. Box 665
St. Charles, MO 63302

Computer Software

PERFECT PROGRAMS

☆ Want to avoid the high cost of computer software? Then why not try some of the great shareware programs that are available? The **CMC Software Sampler** is a software collection for IBM and IBM/compatible users. It contains 15 programs including utilities, games, and screen savers for less than 17 cents each.

Send: $2.50 P&H

Ask For: CMC Software Sampler

Mail To: CMC Development
Dept. FTK27
P.O. Box 1709
Norwalk, CA 90651-1709

Spik-It Spouts

POUR ADVICE

☆ Tired of those messy milk carton spills? Take a tip: Order **a pair of "Spik-it" pour spouts** for those stubborn cardboard cartons that always seem to pour inaccurately. These durable plastic gadgets screw into your carton to provide accurate "pour control." They'll be a big help with little hands when snack time rolls around.

Send: $1.75 P&H

Ask For: Two "Spik-it" Pourers

Mail To: Jay Products, Dept. 1
P.O. Box 10726
Naples, FL 33941

Storybooks

DINOSAUR TALES

☆ With "Jurassic Park" and the Flintstones seemingly everywhere, youngsters have a keen interest in prehistoric times. That's one reason they'll find the wonderful stories in **"Little Dinosaur Adventures"** so interesting. These terrific storybooks make a great diversion for your kindergarten or first-grade class.

Send: $2.00 P&H

Ask For: Two Little Dinosaur Adventures Storybooks

Mail To: Jaye Products, Inc.
Dept. LDA
Books & Crafts
P.O. Box 61471
Fort Myers, FL 33906-1471

Canoeing & Water Safety
UP THE CREEK

☆ If you're located near rivers, lakes, and streams, it's important that your students know something about canoeing and water safety. That's one good reason to order the free booklet **"Welcome Paddler"** from the United States Canoe Association. It's packed with valuable information on everything from dealing with wind and waves to what kind of safety equipment to bring along on that canoe trip.

Send: A long SASE

Ask For: "Welcome Paddler" Canoe Safety Brochure

Mail To: United States Canoe Association
606 Ross St.
Middleton, OH 45044-5062

Personal History Newsletter
THE WAY WE WERE

☆ Everyone has a story to tell and memories worth preserving. That's what Memories Plus, a business dedicated to promoting the writing of personal and family biographies, strongly believes. To help anyone who shares this philosophy, Memories Plus will send a free sample issue of the **"Personal History Newsletter."** Each issue of this monthly four-page publication is filled with suggested writing activities and tips to assist you and your students in compiling an autobiography.

Send: A long SASE

Ask For: Personal History Newsletter

Mail To: Memories Plus
P.O. Box 1339
Albany, OR 97321

Colonial Parchments

PATRIOTIC PAPERS

☆ Instill students with a sense of pride for our country's founders by introducing these **Colonial History Parchments.** Select from a reproduction of George Washington's Call to Arms or a pictorial history of the American Flag. Each parchment looks authentically old and measures 14" x 16".

Send: $2.00 P&H for one; $3.00 for two

Ask For: Parchment (indicate Call and/or Flag)

Mail To: S&H Trading Co.
1187 Coast Village Rd., #208
Montecito, CA 93108-2794

Newsletter Offer

QUILT NEWS

☆ Putting together a magazine is a lot like making a quilt. And by the looks of their professionally produced publication, the authors of The Quilt Peddler know a lot about both. You and your students can learn more about quilting when you order **a free issue of *The Quilt Peddler*.** This 12-page publication covers everything from free offers to free patterns with a list of quilt supply sources thrown in for good measure.

Send: Your name & address on a 3" x 5" card plus a long SASE with two first-class stamps

Ask For: Sample Issue of *The Quilt Peddler*

Mail To: The Quilt Peddler Newsletter Offer
P.O. Box 1485
Valparaiso, IN 46384-1485

Bilingual Coloring Book

COLORFUL LEARNING

☆ Students can keep busy and sharpen their foreign language skills at the same time with this **Moms and Dads/ Mamis y Papis Bilingual Coloring Book.** The text comes in both Spanish and English so that students pick up foreign phrases and improve their vocabularies. This is a terrific way to become familiar with America's second language.

Send: $2.00 P&H

Ask For: Bilingual Coloring Book

Mail To: BUENO, DEPT. FFT
29481 Manzanita Dr.
Campo, CA 91906

Hand-Marbled Bookmarks

LITERARY ART

☆ Chandler Designs Ltd., specializing in picture framing, paper decoration, and printmaking, is a company looking to make its mark in the art world. To that goal, they are giving away **six free hand-marbled bookmarks.** Paper marbling is a centuries-old process used to create beautiful swirling multicolored images on specially treated paper. In addition to the bookmarks, you'll get information on how this process is used on picture frames.

Send: A long SASE

Ask For: Six Free Bookmarks

Mail To: Chandler Designs Ltd.
9017 Mendenhall Ct., Ste. A
Columbia, MD 21045

Historic Postcard
HAIL TO THE CHIEFS

☆ When the Richard Nixon Library was dedicated in 1990, four former Presidents and their wives were on hand to join in the festivities. A photo of this is available on a **5" x 7" postcard of the Historic Meeting of Past Presidents.** Included are Presidents Nixon, Bush, Ford, and Reagan. Since President Nixon's passing, these collector's items have increased in value.

Send: $1.75 for one; $3.00 for two
Ask For: Presidents Postcard
Mail To: United Marketing & Research Co.
9582 Hamilton Ave., Ste. 368
Huntington Beach, CA 92646

Multimedia Computing Booklet
TURN ON TO LEARN

☆ The challenge of education is to move forward. But textbooks and references become dated almost as soon as they're released, and large classes sometimes make it impossible for teachers to give individual attention. That's why Microsoft and the Computer Learning Foundation have authored **"The Power of Learning with Multimedia Personal Computing," a free 13-page booklet.** It illustrates how computers at home, in school, and at the library can enhance the learning process.

Phone: 1-800-426-9400
Ask For: Multimedia Booklet

Story of Banks
BANK ON IT

☆ Two free publications from the Federal Reserve Bank of New York will help you and your students understand banking and foreign trade. **"The Story of Banks"** is a 24-page educational comic book that depicts three young entrepreneurs using various commercial bank services. **"The Basics of Foreign Trade & Exchange"** is a 48-page book that explains some of the key principles of international commerce.

Send: Your name & address

Ask For: Story of Banks and/ or Basics of Foreign Trade & Exchange

Mail To: Federal Reserve Bank of New York
Public Information Dept.
33 Liberty St.
New York, NY 10045

Limit: One copy of each per address

Women's Health Information
HEALTHY FE-MAIL

☆ As a part of the American Health Association's national Women's Health Matters campaign, an informative free booklet titled **"My Health Matters"** is being distributed through a toll-free phone number. The 10-panel guide offers sensitive advice for talking to doctors on matters of sexual health. Serious concerns regarding reproductive tract infections are also addressed.

Phone: 1-800-972-8500

Ask For: My Health Matters Leaflet

FREEBIES FOR TEACHERS **37**

Affordable Choices

THERE'S AFFORD IN YOUR FUTURE

☆ The newest newsletter dealing with money-saving tips is available to you free of charge when you order **a sample issue of *Affordable Choices*.** It's an attractively designed publication for people who want to get more value for their time, energy, and money. And the last time we checked, this certainly describes teachers.

Send: A long SASE

Ask For: Sample Issue of *Affordable Choices*

Mail To: Affordable Choices
P.O. Box 23274
Tigard, OR 97281

Home Security Tips

BURGLAR PROOF

☆ If you're like most teachers, you probably do a good amount of work at home. This means you need a home office or a workshop with a number of important items. Here's a way to protect your valuables without spending a ton of money for a home security system. The Newent Co. will send you a **free sample of its informative newsletter** and offers on other crime deterrents.

Send: A long SASE

Ask For: Security Tips Newsletter

Mail To: The Newent Co. Newsletter
P.O. Box 40
Canterbury, CT 06331

Limit: One per address

Health Information
HAPPY & HEALTHY

☆ If you teach kindergarten, the lower grades, or work in a child care center, check out this great free offer from Dixie. The Dixie Child Care Challenge will provide you with a **cold-proofing teacher's kit** that includes a series of lessons, exercises, stickers, and puppets to help get the message across about how to stay healthy during cold & flu season. This kit is for groups of 10 or more and is available through June, 1995, or while supplies last.

Send: Your name, address, and class size

Ask For: Dixie Child Care Teachers Kit

Mail To: Dixie Child Care Challenge
625 N. Michigan Ave., Ste. 2400-K
Chicago, IL 60611

Baking Recipes
SWAN CELEBRATION

☆ In celebration of the 100th anniversary of Swan's Down flour, you can get a special collection of 20 fabulous recipes by Rose Beranbaum in the **Swan's Down Best Baking Booklet.** Ms. Beranbaum is also the author of the award-winning cookbook "The Cake Bible," so using this for cooking class projects is sure to satisfy anyone's sweet tooth.

Send: $1.00 P&H

Ask For: Swan's Down Best Baking Booklet

Mail To: Swan's Down 100th Booklet
P.O. Box 60296
New Orleans, LA 70160-0296

Diet Supplement

GARLIC BENEFIT

Kyolic, Ltd.

☆ Recent scientific reports have proved that garlic offers several health benefits, but taking garlic in its raw form has obvious drawbacks. Fortunately, there's Kyolic and Kyo-Chrome Aged Garlic Extracts. These dietary supplements offer the beneficial compounds of garlic in odorless caplets. If you would like more information and **free trial size packets of Kyolic and Kyo-Chrome,** write away today.

Send: Your name & address

Ask For: Kyolic & Kyo-Chrome Samples

Mail To: Kyolic
c/o H/K Communications
244 Madison Ave., #9H
New York, NY 10016

Dry Skin Information

DRY NO MORE

☆ If playground duty is causing you to suffer from dry skin, you're probably looking for solutions to the problem. **"The Dry Skin Answer Book"** is a free brochure that contains an interview with Dr. Nelson Novick, a dermatologist and author of several books on skin care. You'll also receive a money-saving coupon for Curel Therapeutic Moisturizing Lotion.

Phone: 1-800-3-DRY-SKIN

Ask For: The Dry Skin Answer Book

Animal & Earth Awareness

BE KIND

☆ Everyone needs to learn to be kind to animals and protect the environment. Find out how and why by reading a free copy of **KIND News,** which is prepared in reading levels for kindergarten through second grades, for third and fourth grades, and for fifth- and sixth-grade students. You'll also receive a free **Student Action Guide** to help you launch an Earth/Animal Protection Club.

Send: Your name & address

Ask For: *KIND News* (indicate grade level) & Student Action Guide

Mail To: N.A.H.E.E.
P.O. Box 362: Dept. FF
East Haddam, CT 06423-0362

Asthma Information

BREATHE EASIER

☆ If you have students who suffer from asthma-like allergies, or if this is a condition you are personally familiar with, you may be able to breathe easier this season. Call for your **free Guide to Asthma and Allergies.** This eight-page booklet explains the connection between asthma and allergies. It provides helpful information and hints on dealing with asthma, as well as money-saving coupons toward the purchase of Primatene Mist.

Phone: 1-800-PRIMATENE

Ask For: Guide to Asthma and Allergies

BeSure Sample

DON'T GAS

☆ Now you can eat beans and vegetables with the confidence that you won't suffer embarrassing flatulence. BeSure capsules provide a simple all-natural food enzyme that, when taken before meals, eliminates intestinal gas before it starts. It's allergy safe and can be taken with either hot or cold foods. Send for your **free samples of BeSure capsules.**

Send: Your name & address

Ask For: BeSure Sample

Mail To: BeSure
c/o HK Communications
244 Madison Ave., #9H
New York, NY 10016

Forecast Booklet

WEATHER OR NOT

☆ You don't need satellite photos and a degree in meteorology to be able to tell what kind of weather is coming. But you do need a copy of **"How to Forecast the Weather,"** a colorful pamphlet that gives you an idea of what weather to expect by looking at the morning skies, checking out the wind, and analyzing cloud patterns.

Send: $1.00 P&H

Ask For: How to Forecast the Weather

Mail To: Cloud Chart, Inc.
P.O. Box 21298
Charleston, SC 29413

Citrus Fruit Information

SWEET AS THE SUN

☆ Most people like to enjoy a cold glass of orange juice or to take a bite of a juicy tangerine. But there are many other ways to enjoy these tropical fruit delights. Order two new free booklets from Sunkist entitled **"Sunkist Tangerine Treasures" and "Sunkist Navels: The Favorite Eating Orange."** Both are filled with recipes, information, and tips on enjoying these popular citrus fruits.

Send: A long SASE with two first-class stamps

Ask For: Sunkist Navel Orange/Tangerine Booklets

Mail To: Sunkist Growers, Inc.
Dept. Navel or Tang
P.O. Box 788
Van Nuys, CA 91409-7888

Sign Language Guide

KEEP QUIET

☆ Did you know that English and Spanish are the two most used languages in the Americas? But did you realize that third on the list is sign language? Help familiarize your students with signing by ordering **this set of three Manual Alphabet Poster Postcards.** They contain all the sign language letters of the alphabet.

Send: $1.00 P&H

Ask For: Sign Language Postcards

Mail To: Keep Quiet
P.O. Box 367
Stanhope, NJ 07874

American Harvest Newsletter

GARDEN FRESH

☆ You may teach a gardening class or you may teach nutrition. In either case, your students will enjoy reading a recent issue of the **American Harvest Newsletter,** a publication devoted to celebrating the fresh fruits and vegetables harvested from America's gardens. Beyond information that will help you develop some new green thumbs, there's also some tasty recipes.

Send: $2.00 P&H

Ask For: *American Harvest Newsletter* Sample

Mail To: Cornucopia Press
3 Golf Center, Ste. 221
Hoffman Estates, IL 60195

Potluck Party Planner

POPULAR PARTY

☆ One of the most popular ideas for a classroom celebration is a potluck party for which each student brings a different dish from home. Parkay Margarine has discovered that people love potlucks because they're both easy and economical. That's why they've put together this **free Potluck Party Planner.** It will take the guesswork out of the planning process and help you stage a great event. This offer is good until August, 1995, or while supplies last.

Send: A long SASE

Ask For: Potluck Party Planner

Mail To: Potluck Party Planner
55 Union St.
San Francisco, CA 94111

Collector's Newsletter

COLLECTION TIME

☆ Most students and teachers have been exposed to the world of collectibles and its wide variety of choices. Be it coins, stamps, trading cards, or comic books, there's information on how to add to personal collections in your free issue of **Collectors' Classified.** This newsletter also runs feature ads for both dealers and collectors around the country. While sparking your students' interests, you might even find time to start a hobby of your own.

Send: Your name & address

Ask For: Free Copy of *Collectors' Classified*

Mail To: Collectors' Classified
P.O. Box 347
Holbrook, MA 02343-0347F

Bath Oil Sample

YOU NEED THERAPY

☆ After a long day of pacing around the classroom and schoolyard, you need a little relaxation. The Good Earth aromatherapy products are designed to nurture you on the inside as well as the outside by inspiring relaxation and a sense of well-being. Try a **1-oz. sample of Body, Bath & Massage Oil** and experience the wonderful restorative benefits of aromatherapy.

Send: $2.00 P&H

Ask For: Sample Body, Bath & Massage Oil

Mail To: The Good Earth Store
P.O. Box 129
Liverpool, NY 13088

Needlecraft Kit

SEW WHAT NOW?

☆ Stop feeling needled for something new to introduce to your class. A **Quicksew Needlecraft Kit** is a great way to pass some time with an interesting crafts project. The kit comes with its own needle, yarn, and a 6" x 8" canvas with a color printed pattern chosen by the supplier from a variety of homey designs like flowers and animals.

Send: $1.00 P&H

Ask For: Quicksew Needlecraft Kit

Mail To: Surprise Gift of the Month
55 Railroad Ave.
Garnerville, NY 10923

Kamora Culinary Club

FOR ADULTS ONLY

☆ Teachers spend time with kids all day long. Once you get home you might enjoy some delightful adult drinks and entrees that have just a hint of Kamora Coffee Liqueur in the mix. For a collection of recipes and entertaining tips, join the **Kamora Culinary Club** free. You'll receive the club's quarterly newsletter, "Concoctions," which will give you some good ideas on how to add a little kick to your recipes. You must be 21 or older to respond to this offer.

Send: Your name & Address

Ask For: Kamora Culinary Club Membership

Mail To: Kamora Culinary Club
P.O. Box 5004
Ronko, PA 17573

Sweepstakes Tips

SWEEP UP

☆ Try your luck. It doesn't cost much. Just a stamp and a little time. Who knows, you could be that one in a million lucky winner. Actually, your odds of winning sweepstakes are greatly enhanced when you order a free sample copy of **Sweeping the USA,** a newsletter devoted to sweepstakes. It comes filled with information on great sweepstakes promotions and good ideas on how to become a consistent winner.

Send: Two first-class stamps

Ask For: *Sweeping the USA* Sample Copy

Mail To: Delosh
171 Water St.
Massena, NY 13662

Christmas Parchment

WHERE'S SANTA?

☆ *Harper's Weekly* first published the classic *"Seeing Santa Claus"* in its December, 1876, edition. It features a charming illustration of a young boy on a roof spying Santa going down the chimney. This poster-size, antique-looking parchment makes a great Yuletide decoration for the classroom or a stocking stuffer for your own kids.

Send: $2.00 P&H for one; $3.00 for two

Ask For: Seeing Santa

Mail To: S&H Trading Company
1187 Coast Village Rd. #208
Montecito, CA 93108

Wonder Walkers

A CUSHY LIFE

☆ You're probably on your feet most of the day. How would you like to soften the blow when you march from class to class, then head out to the schoolyard for recess? Order **a pair of Wonder Walkers,** the shock-absorbing insoles that will make your life a little easier and your feet a little more comfortable. They not only provide cushioning comfort, but they help protect your feet, legs, and back from injury.

Send: $1.00 P&H

Ask For: Wonder Walkers Insoles (include desired shoe size)

Mail To: Benchmark Brands, Inc.
3943 Delp Rd.
Memphis, TN 38118

Klutch Sample

A MOUTHFUL

☆ It's not heavily advertised, but the word of mouth from denture wearers has been great for over 65 years. See for yourself what all the talk is about with a **free sample of Klutch denture adhesive powder.** Made of natural ingredients, it provides comfortable superholding power without strong taste. This trial-size packet also comes with a 25-cent coupon toward a purchase of Klutch.

Send: A long SASE

Ask For: Sample Packet of Klutch

Mail To: I. Putnam, Inc.
Dept. FB94
P.O. Box 444
Big Flats, NY 14814

Vacation Ideas
HIT THE ROAD

☆ After spending the year locked in a classroom, you can't wait for vacation time to roll around. But it gets harder and harder to decide on the right place to get away from it all. Try reading through **"21 Great Vacation Ideas Your Travel Agent Won't Tell You About!"** This special report and travel book is devoted to out-of-the-ordinary ideas on unique destinations and great vacation activities from scuba diving to bicycle touring.

Send: $1.00 P&H

Ask For: 21 Great Vacation Ideas

Mail To: 21 Great Vacation Ideas
c/o Questing Inc., Dept. 800
24729 Calle Altamira
Calabasas, CA 91302

Swiss-Type Knife
SURVIVAL STUFF

☆ It's a jungle out there, so you need everything you can get to help you survive. One handy tool is this **Swiss-type army knife.** It has five functions—scissors, toothpick, nail file, tweezer, and high-carbon stainless blade. Yet when folded, it's only 2¼" long—small enough to fit on a key ring or throw in a briefcase or purse.

Send: $2.00 P&H for one; $3.50 for two

Ask For: Swiss-Type Army Knife

Mail To: S&H Trading Co.
1187 Coast Village Rd. #208
Montecito, CA 93108-2794

Parchment Posters
PATRIOTIC POSTERS

☆ In addition to your lessons on history and civics, why not decorate your classroom bulletin board with one or both of these **patriotic posters** that measure approximately 14" x 16" and are printed on antique-look parchment? The Presidents Poster has pictures of all 42 Presidents, their names, years in office, and a reproduction of their signatures. The "Star-Spangled Banner" is a reprint of the national anthem in Francis Scott Key's handwriting and also has illustrations and a brief historical account of the moment our anthem was penned.

Send: $2.00 P&H each; $3.00 for two
Ask For: Presidents and/or Banner Parchment
Mail To: S&H Trading Co.
1187 Coast Village Rd. #208
Montecito, CA 93108-2794

Sample Seeds
EXOTIC GARDEN

☆ You don't have to travel the world gathering exotic seeds to create a world-class garden. Just request a **free packet of exotic seeds** from this company offering over a thousand varieties of exotic, tropical, and unusual seeds. Your free sample package will be selected at random and will carry a short description of the plant with growing instructions.

Send: Your name & address
Ask For: Free Exotic Seeds
Mail To: Free Exotic Seeds
3421 Bream St.
Gautier, MS 39553

Stock Exchange Brochure

TAKING STOCK

☆ The Dow is up—or is it down? We hear about it every day on the news and read about it in the newspaper. But how much do we really know about the inner workings of the stock exchange? You'll know a lot more when you send for **"Journey Through a Stock Exchange."** This colorful booklet is in a comic book format, but it's no joke. It tells you and your students all about how the stock market works.

Send: $1.00 P&H

Ask For: Journey through a Stock Exchange

Mail To: American Stock Exchange
Publications Dept.
86 Trinity Place
New York, NY 10006

Fat-Free Tips

CHEW THE FAT

☆ Let's chew the fat about fat. **The Fat-Free Exchange** publishes a newsletter featuring recipes and tips on how to trim the fat in your diet, and it wants you to have a free issue. This four-page monthly publication is designed to let readers swap fat-cutting hints and recipes. There's also information on exercise and weight control.

Send: A long SASE

Ask For: Fat-Free Newsletter Sample Copy

Mail To: The Fat-Free Exchange
7334 Panache Way
Boca Raton, FL 33433

Recipe Leaflets

GOOD EATING

☆ Two things add something special to a meal: a tasty side dish and a special dessert. Order these two free leaflets and you and your students will get recipe ideas for both. **"Cheese Makes It Better" and "Recipes for Sensational Desserts"** are enough to make your mouth water. How does a chocolate pecan tart sound? Or maybe a cheese lover's Sloppy Joe? Let's eat!

Send: A long SASE

Ask For: Cheese Makes It Better/ Sensational Dessert Recipe Leaflets

Mail To: National Dairy Board
c/o Lewis & Neale, Inc.-FR5
928 Broadway, Room 600
New York, NY 10010

FAN-tastic Freebies

☆ Most professional sports franchises have free materials, such as season schedules and ticket information, that they give away to enthusiastic fans. Some teams even give away fan packages that may contain stickers, photos, fan club information, catalogs, and more.

To get these great items, all you need to do is write to the Public Relations office of your favorite team, include your name and address, then ask for a "fan package."

We've compiled the addresses of all the professional baseball, basketball, football, and hockey teams. Although not all teams require it, we recommend you send a long SASE to help speed your request. Be sure to remember that mail to

Canada requires extra postage. Postage rates are changing, so check with your local Post Office for the current rate.

Here's another tip: If you want to contact a specific player on your or your students' favorite team, address the envelope to his attention. Keep in mind that because of the high volume of fan mail some players and each team receives, it may take eight weeks or more for a response.

AMERICAN LEAGUE BASEBALL TEAMS

Baltimore Orioles
333 West Camden St.
Baltimore, MD 21201

Boston Red Sox
4 Yawkey Way
Boston, MA 02115

California Angels
P.O. Box 2000
Anaheim, CA 92803

Chicago White Sox
333 W. 35th St.
Chicago, IL 60616

Cleveland Indians
Jacobs Field
2401 Ontario St.
Cleveland, OH 44115

Detroit Tigers
Tiger Stadium
Detroit, MI 48216

Kansas City Royals
P.O. Box 419969
Kansas City, MO 64141

Milwaukee Brewers
201 S. 46th St.
Milwaukee, WI 53214

Minnesota Twins
501 Chicago Ave. South
Minneapolis, MN 55415

New York Yankees
Yankee Stadium
Bronx, NY 10451

Oakland Athletics
Oakland Coliseum
Oakland, CA 94621

Seattle Mariners
P.O. Box 4100
Seattle, WA 98104

Texas Rangers
The Ballpark in Arlington
P.O. Box 90111
Arlington, TX 76004

Toronto Blue Jays
SkyDome
One Blue Jay Way
Ste. 3200
Toronto, Ontario,
Canada M5V 1J1
(Note: first-class mail to Canada requires extra stamps)

NATIONAL LEAGUE BASEBALL TEAMS

Atlanta Braves
P.O. Box 4064
Atlanta, GA 30302

Chicago Cubs
Wrigley Field
1060 West Addison St.
Chicago, IL 60613

Cincinnati Reds
100 Riverfront Stadium
Cincinnati, OH 45202

Colorado Rockies
1700 Broadway, Ste. 2100
Denver, CO 80290

Florida Marlins
2267 N.W. 199th St.
Miami, FL 33056

Houston Astros
P.O. Box 288
Houston, TX 77001

Los Angeles Dodgers
1000 Elysian Park Ave.
Los Angeles, CA 90012

Montreal Expos
P.O. Box 500
Station M
Montreal, Quebec,
Canada H1V 3P2
(Note: first-class mail to Canada requires extra stamps)

New York Mets
Shea Stadium
Flushing, NY 11368

Philadelphia Phillies
P.O. Box 7575
Philadelphia, PA 19101

Pittsburgh Pirates
P.O. Box 7000
Pittsburgh, PA 15212

St. Louis Cardinals
250 Stadium Plaza
St. Louis, MO 63102

San Diego Padres
P.O. Box 2000
San Diego, CA 92112

San Francisco Giants
Candlestick Park
San Francisco, CA 94124

NATIONAL BASKETBALL ASSOCIATION TEAMS

Atlanta Hawks
One CNN Center
South Tower, Ste. 405
Atlanta, GA 30303

Boston Celtics
151 Merrimac St.
5th Floor
Boston, MA 02114

Charlotte Hornets
One Hive Dr.
Charlotte, NC 28217

Chicago Bulls
One Magnificent Mile
980 N. Michigan Ave.
Ste. 1600
Chicago, IL 60611

Cleveland Cavaliers
2923 Streetsboro Rd.
Richfield, OH 44286

Dallas Mavericks
Reunion Arena
777 Sports St.
Dallas, TX 75207

Denver Nuggets
1635 Clay St.
Denver, CO 75207

Detroit Pistons
The Palace of Auburn Hills
Two Championship Dr.
Auburn Hills, MI 48326

Golden State Warriors
Oakland Coliseum Arena
Oakland, CA 94621

Houston Rockets
The Summit
10 Greenway Plaza
Houston, TX 77046

Indiana Pacers
300 East Market St.
Indianapolis, IN 46204

Los Angeles Clippers
L.A. Sports Arena
3939 S. Figueroa St.
Los Angeles, CA 90037

Los Angeles Lakers
Great Western Forum
3900 W. Manchester Blvd.
Inglewood, CA 90306

Miami Heat
Miami Arena
Miami, FL 33136

Milwaukee Bucks
Bradley Center
1001 N. Fourth St.
Milwaukee, WI 53203

Minnesota Timberwolves
Target Center
600 First Ave. North
Minneapolis, MN 55403

New Jersey Nets
Meadowlands Arena
East Rutherford, NJ 07073

New York Knickerbockers
Madison Square Garden
2 Penn Plaza, 3rd Floor
New York, NY 10121

Orlando Magic
Orlando Arena
1 Magic Place
Orlando, FL 32801

Philadelphia 76ers
Veterans Stadium
Broad St. & Pattison Ave.
Philadelphia, PA 19148

Phoenix Suns
P.O. Box 1369
Phoenix, AZ 85001

Portland Trail Blazers
Suite 600 Lloyd Building
700 N.E. Multnomah St.
Portland, OR 97232

Sacramento Kings
One Sports Pkwy.
Sacramento, CA 95834

San Antonio Spurs
Alamodome
100 Montana St.
San Antonio, TX 78203

Seattle Supersonics
190 Queene Anne Ave. North
Ste. 200
Seattle, WA 98109

Toronto Raptors
150 York St., Ste. 1100
Toronto, Ontario,
Canada M5H3S5
(Note: first-class mail to Canada requires extra stamps)

Utah Jazz
Delta Center
301 West South Temple
Salt Lake City, UT 84101

Vancouver Grizzlies
NBA Vancouver
780 Beatty St., 3rd Fl.
Vancouver, British Columbia,
Canada V6B2M1
(Note: first-class mail to Canada requires extra stamps)

Washington Bullets
One Harry S. Truman Dr.
Landover, MD 20785

AMERICAN CONFERENCE FOOTBALL TEAMS

Buffalo Bills
One Bills Dr.
Orchard Park, NY 14127

Cincinnati Bengals
200 Riverfront Stadium
Cincinnati, OH 45202

Cleveland Browns
80 First Ave.
Berea, OH 44017

Denver Broncos
13655 Broncos Pkwy.
Englewood, CO 80112

Houston Oilers
6910 Fannin St.
Houston, TX 77030

Indianapolis Colts
P.O. Box 535000
Indianaplis, IN 46253

Kansas City Chiefs
One Arrowhead Dr.
Kansas City, MO 64129

Los Angeles Raiders
332 Center St.
El Segundo, CA 90245

Miami Dolphins
Joe Robbie Stadium
2269 NW 199th St.
Miami, FL 33056

New England Patriots
Foxboro Stadium
Route 1
Foxboro, MA 02035

New York Jets
1000 Fulton Ave.
Hempstead, NY 11550

Pittsburgh Steelers
300 Stadium Circle
Pittsburgh, PA 15212

San Diego Chargers
P.O. Box 609609
San Diego, CA 92160

Seattle Seahawks
11220 NE 53rd St.
Kirkland, WA 98033

NATIONAL FOOTBALL CONFERENCE TEAMS

Arizona Cardinals
P.O. Box 888
Phoenix, AZ 85001

Atlanta Falcons
2745 Burnett Rd.
Suwanee, GA 30174

Chicago Bears
Halas Hall
250 N. Washington
Lake Forest, IL 60045

Dallas Cowboys
Cowboys Center
One Cowboys Pkwy.
Irving, TX 75063

Detroit Lions
Pontiac Silverdome
1200 Featherstone Rd.
Pontiac, MI 48342

Green Bay Packers
1265 Lombardi Ave.
Green Bay, WI 54307

Los Angeles Rams
2327 West Lincoln Ave.
Anaheim, CA 92801

Minnesota Vikings
9520 Viking Dr.
Eden Prairie, MN 55344

New Orleans Saints
6928 Saints Dr.
Metairie, LA 70003

New York Giants
Giants Stadium
East Rutherford, NJ 07073

Philadelphia Eagles
Veterans Stadium
Broad St. & Pattison Ave.
Philadelphia, PA 19148

San Francisco 49ers
4949 Centennial Blvd.
Santa Clara, CA 95054

Tampa Bay Buccaneers
1 Buccaneer Place
Tampa, FL 33607

Washington Redskins
21300 Redskin Park Dr.
Ashburn, WA 22011

NATIONAL FOOTBALL LEAGUE EXPANSION TEAMS

Carolina Panthers
227 West Trade St.
Ste. #1600
Charlotte, NC 28202

Jacksonville Jaguars
1 Stadium Place
Jacksonville, FL 32202

NATIONAL HOCKEY LEAGUE TEAMS

Anaheim Mighty Ducks
The Pond
P.O. Box 61077
Anaheim, CA 92803

Boston Bruins
Boston Garden
150 Causeway St.
Boston, MA 02114

Buffalo Sabres
Memorial Auditorium
140 Main St.
Buffalo, NY 14202

Chicago Blackhawks
1901 West Madison St.
Chicago, IL 60612

Calgary Flames
Olympic Saddledome
P.O. Box 1540, Station M
Calgary, Alberta,
Canada T2P 3B9
(Note: first-class mail to Canada requires extra stamps)

Dallas Stars
901 Main St.
Ste. 2301
Dallas, TX 75202

Detroit Red Wings
Joe Louis Arena
600 Civic Center Dr.
Detroit, MI 48226

Edmonton Oilers
Northlands Coliseum
74241 118th Ave.
Edmonton, Alberta,
Canada T5B 4M9
(Note: first-class mail to Canada requires extra stamps)

Florida Panthers
100 North East Third Ave.
10th Floor
Ft. Lauderdale, FL 33301

Hartford Whalers
242 Trumbull St., 8th Fl.
Hartford, CT 06103

Los Angeles Kings
Great Western Forum
3900 West Manchester Blvd.
Inglewood, CA 90306

Montreal Canadiens
Montreal Forum
2313 St. Catherine St. West
Montreal, Quebec,
Canada H3H 1N2
(Note: first-class mail to Canada requires extra stamps)

New Jersey Devils
Meadowlands Arena
P.O. Box 504
East Rutherford, NJ 07073

New York Islanders
Nassau Veteran's
Memorial Coliseum
Uniondale, NY 11553

New York Rangers
4 Penn Plaza, 4th Fl.
New York, NY 10001

Ottawa Senators
301 Moodie Dr., Ste. 200
Nepean, Ontario,
Canada K2H 9C4
(Note: first-class mail to Canada requires extra stamps)

Philadelphia Flyers
The Spectrum
Pattison Place
Philadelphia, PA 19148

Pittsburgh Penguins
Civic Arena
Pittsburgh, PA 15219

Quebec Nordiques
Colisee de Quebec
2205 Avenue du Colisee
Quebec City, Quebec,
Canada G1L 4W7
(Note: first-class mail to Canada requires extra stamps)

St. Louis Blues
St. Louis Arena
5700 Oakland Ave.
St. Louis, MO 63110

San Jose Sharks
525 West Santa Clara St.
San Jose, CA 95113

Tampa Bay Lightning
501 East Kennedy Blvd.
Ste. 175
Tampa, FL 33602

Toronto Maple Leafs
Maple Leafs garden
60 Carlton St.
Toronto, Ontario,
Canada M5B 1L1
(Note: first-class mail to Canada requires extra stamps)

Vancouver Canucks
Pacific Coliseum
100 North Renfrew St.
Vancouver, British Columbia,
Canada V5K 3N7
(Note: first-class mail to Canada requires extra stamps)

Washington Capitals
USAir Arena
Landover, MD 20785

Winnipeg Jets
Winnipeg Arena
15-1430 Maroons Rd.
Winnipeg, Manitoba,
Canada R3G 0L5
(Note: first-class mail to Canada requires extra stamps)

Computer Buyers Guide
SMART SHOPPING

☆ With almost daily advances in computer technology, buying a home PC can be a tricky proposition, even for experts. You can help yourself and your students decide exactly what type of hardware, software, and accessories are needed in order to get the most out of home computing. **The Guide to Buying an IBM/Compatible** discusses monitors, printers, scanners, and various programs. You'll also get a coupon for a computer tutorial disk.

Send: $2.00 P&H

Ask For: Guide to Buying an IBM/Compatible, Software, and Accessories

Mail To: Computer Kingdom
Freebies Buying Guide
P.O. Box 3002
Providence, RI 02906

Finland Films
FINNISH LINE

☆ If you didn't know that Finland is the northernmost democracy in the world, and a beautiful country dotted with lakes, rivers, forests, and beautiful villages, then you need to order **Films of the Nations.** This free catalog of educational videos and films of Finland also comes with printed material that will help you teach your next geography lesson with up-to-date information.

Send: Your name & address

Ask For: Films of the Nations/Finland Booklets

Mail To: Films of the Nations
Box 449
Clarksburg, NJ 08510

Magazine
PLAYING FOR KEEPS

☆ Searching for a way to increase your students' reading ability, confidence, and general interest in school? Check out a sample issue of **Plays, The Drama Magazine for Young People.** Each issue includes 8–10 new plays, arranged by age level (lower grades through high school). You'll find modern and traditional comedies along with dramas, monologues, and puppet plays, all written with easy-to-follow production notes for flexible casting.

Send: $2.00 P&H

Ask For: Sample Issue of *Plays, The Drama Magazine for Young People*

Mail To: Plays, Inc.
120 Boylston St.
Boston, MA 02116-4615

Eye Information
VISIONARY

☆ Did you know that poor vision is very often mistaken for learning disabilities? The **free brochure Your Child's Eyes,** developed by the American Academy of Pediatrics, explains this and much more. Learn about common visual problems, how to detect them, and the normal treatment for such ailments. Valuable free information.

Send: A long SASE

Ask For: *Your Child's Eyes* Brochure

Mail To: American Academy of Pediatrics
Dept. C-Your Child's Eyes
P.O. Box 927
141 Northwest Point Blvd.
Elk Grove Village, IL 60009-0927

Magazine

SOMETHING FOR NOTHING

☆ Can you or your class use fun items such as rulers, stickers, fun pencils, novelty erasers, holiday craft projects, and more? Can you use educational items and informative publications? Then you need **FREEBIES Magazine.** Each issue features approximately 100 useful, informative, fun, and seasonal items that are available for free or for a small postage and handling charge.

Send: $2.00 P&H for one sample issue; $4.95 for a one-year, five-issue subscription (regular rate is $8.95)

Ask For: Sample Issue of *FREEBIES* or a One-year Subscription as indicated above

Mail To: FREEBIES/Teacher Offer
1135 Eugenia Place
P.O. Box 5025
Carpinteria, CA 93014

Information and Catalog

FOR THE BIRDS

☆ When treated with care, the birds surrounding your home or schoolyard can be fun to watch. Your free copy of **Bird Feeding Tips** from Droll Yankees illustrates the best feeding stations to watch birds eat, along with brief descriptions of each bird.

Send: Your name & address

Ask For: *Bird Feeding Tips*

Mail To: Droll Yankees, Inc.
27 Mill Road, Dept. SC
Foster, RI 02825

Historical Information
TIME TRAVEL

☆ Expose your students to American history without opening a textbook. Receive free information about Charleston, South Carolina's, **Old Exchange Building** and carry your classroom back in time. Discuss the American Revolution when this building acted as headquarters for the British and held American patriots in the dungeon. Then there were the peaceful years when George Washington held gala receptions in its halls.

Send: A long SASE
Ask For: Information on the Old Exchange Building
Mail To: The Old Exchange and Provost Dungeon
122 East Bay at Broad St.
Charleston, SC 29401

Teaching Fire Safety
LETHAL LESSON

☆ Fire prevention lessons involve more than just admonishing students not to play with matches. **Teaching Fire Safety to Kids** is a free pamphlet that tells you how to counsel and educate children who play with fire. If you don't think this is a big problem, consider the fact that 45% of school-age children are reported as having played with matches at least once and 21% have actually set fires.

Send: Your name & address
Ask For: *Teaching Fire Safety to Kids* Brochure
Mail To: National Institute for Burn Medicine
909 E. Ann St.
Ann Arbor, MI 48104

Stop Scalds Flyer

BOILING OVER

☆ If you can prevent students and your own family members from scalding themselves, not only will you save them unnecessary pain, but you can also save them big money in hospital care. That sounds like a great deal, so order **Be Smart: Stop Scalds.** This simple flyer is free and is packed with important details on preventing scalding accidents in the kitchen and bathroom.

Send: Your name & address

Ask For: *Be Smart: Stop Scalds* Flyer

Mail To: National Institute for Burn Medicine
909 E. Ann St.
Ann Arbor, MI 48104

Education Film Catalog

FILM STUDIES

☆ Diversify! This is the key to business and teaching. Add the visual aids available from **Business Education Films** to break up lectures and teach students about such real-world business topics as advertising, entrepreneurship, and salesmanship. There are also videos and software to help with test-taking, typing, and vocational guidance. Send for the catalog and get a detailed listing.

Send: Your name & address

Ask For: Business Education Films Catalog

Mail To: Business Education Films
Box 449
Clarksburg, NJ 08510

Skin Cancer Information

OVEREXPOSURE

☆ There was a time when sunbathers didn't think twice about spending all day outside and uncovered. But recent studies have shown that more than 700,000 Americans get skin cancer each year. The best way to play it safe is to be armed with up-to-date information, the very kind available in the free pamphlet **"Skin Cancer: A Growing Threat."**

Send: A long SASE

Ask For: Skin Cancer: A Growing Threat

Mail To: ASCP
Box CRPD-FB
2100 W. Harrison St.
Chicago, IL 60612-3798

Teacher Computer Software

HIGH-TECH HELPER

☆ Teachers need all the help they can get, especially at the reasonable rates of these **three IBM/Compatible software programs.** GradeBook helps you computerize your grading system and data. Test-Maker will keep your examinations current and on the cutting edge. Computer-Assisted Program Creator allows you to design instructional programs for your students. Order one or all three at this low price.

Send: $2.00 P&H for each

Ask For: Gradebook, Test-Maker, and/or Computer-Assisted Program Creator
(indicate 360K or 720K format)

Mail To: Computer Kingdom
P.O. Box 3002
Freebies Teach Offer
Providence, RI 02906

Medical Treatment Form

A MATTER OF CONSENT

☆ Before you embark on a class field trip or even allow students to run around in the schoolyard, it's important to take precautions for their safety. One important item to have on file is this **free Medical Treatment Form,** to be signed by parents or guardians, which lists important information about family physicians and insurance policy numbers.

Send: A long SASE

Ask For: Medical Treatment Form

Mail To: Practical Parenting
Dept. 1/FB-JR
Deephaven, MN 55391

Limit: One per request

Stories/Monologues

GOOD READING

☆ If you teach high school or college-age students, they prefer to read something a bit more challenging than the normal fare. Dimitri Publications is offering three books that are perfect for this age group. **Mona Rogers in Person** is a book of women's monologues, while **Baby Redboots' Revenge** is a collection of monologues for men. **Cigarette Waltz** is a collection of short stories. Order one or all three.

Send: $2.00 P&H for each book

Ask For: Mona Rogers, Baby Redboots', or Cigarette Waltz

Mail To: Galas
2425 First Ave., Ste. T
San Diego, CA 92101

No Smoking Sign
STOP SIGN

☆ Students may think smoking is cool, but it's your job to teach them the truth. As a daily reminder, send for this **free No Smoking Sign** from the American Lung Association and post it on your class bulletin board. It's shaped like a traffic sign and is imprinted with the important message "Lungs at Work . . . No Smoking."

Send: Your name & address
Ask For: No Smoking Sign
Call: 1-800-LUNG USA (800-586-4872)
Mail To: American Lung Association
P.O. Box 596-FB
Pamphlet #0121
New York, NY 10116-0596

Parchment
A TOUCH OF HISTORY

☆ Textbooks are great for teaching American history, but this authentic-looking 14" x 16" antiqued parchment will add to your lesson plan and classroom. The **Declaration of Independence parchment** comes with a painting of the Continental Congress, replicas of the signatures that appeared on the original, and information on the men who signed one of America's most important documents.

Send: $2.00 P&H for one; $3.00 for two
Ask For: Declaration of Independence
Mail To: S&H Trading Company
1187 Coast Village Rd. #208
Montecito, CA 93108

Computer Graphics Software
DESKTOP DESIGNER

☆ Graphic design is not something better left to experts when you have the help of an IBM/compatible computer. If you have a dot matrix or a laser printer, **Create Your Own Greeting Cards, Posters, and Letterhead** is a program you should own. It comes with some terrific clip art libraries at no extra charge, not to mention numerous type styles and special-effect capabilities. This program normally sells for $20, but FREEBIES readers pay only $6.00, a 70% discount!

Send: $6.00 P&H

Ask For: Create Your Own Greeting Cards, Posters, and Letterhead (indicate 360K or 720K format)

Mail To: Computer Kingdom
Freebies Press Offer
P.O. Box 3002
Providence, RI 02906

Luminous Tape
EVER-GLOW

☆ Put this **glow in the dark tape** on classroom light switches for safety, make unique stickers with your students, decorate Halloween costumes, or just take it home and use some for making fishing lures. The possibilities are endless with this 3" x 4" sheet of waterproof luminous tape.

Send: $1.75 P&H

Ask For: Glow in the Dark Tape

Mail To: Esther's E-Z Shop
Dept. GT
P.O. Box 1831
Pomona, CA 91769

HIV and AIDS Information

BETTER SAFE THAN SORRY

☆ Even with all the information concerning HIV and AIDS available through the media, many people are still misinformed about these serious conditions. The best way to avoid contact with the AIDS virus is to be knowledgeable and well versed on all aspects of the subject. **"What You Need to Know about HIV and AIDS"** is just such a resource, and it's free. It will help answer most, if not all, of your students' questions about this serious subject.

Send: A long SASE

Ask For: What You Need to Know about HIV and AIDS

Mail To: ASCP
Box CPRD-FB
2100 W. Harrison St.
Chicago, IL 60612-3798

Christmas Parchment

PARCHED POETRY

☆ **"Twas the night before Christmas"** is the lead on the classic Christmas poem penned by Clement Moore. Since 1823 it has captured the imagination and attention of children eagerly awaiting a visit from Santa. Now you can have a beautiful reproduction of the classic handwritten original verse printed on 11" x 14" antiqued parchment paper. Get your students into the holiday spirit!

Send: $2.00 P&H for one; $3.00 for two

Ask For: Twas

Mail To: S&H Trading Company
1187 Coast Village Rd. #208
Montecito, CA 93108

Recipe Brochure
SAY CHEESE

☆ Nothing adds a special touch to parties or meals like a little cheese. You can teach your aspiring homemakers some great recipes and serving tips for this popular dairy product when you order **"Naturally Entertaining,"** a colorful, informative free brochure. Beyond some ideas on how to put together a cheese buffet or cook up a tasty torte, you'll find out how to match certain cheeses with the right fruits and nuts.

Send:	Your name & address
Ask For:	Naturally Entertaining Brochure
Mail To:	Wisconsin Milk Marketing Board Dept. FRB-4711 8418 Excelsior Dr. Madison, WI 53717

No Smoking Booklet
KIDS SPEAK OUT

☆ It's one thing for you to tell students to stop smoking, but it's something else for them to hear it from their peers. **No Smoking Can Cause a Healthy, Long, and Fulfilling Life** is a free booklet authored by kids. It contains drawings, stories, pictures, and puzzles, all with the same important message—don't smoke!

Send:	Your name & address
Ask For:	No Smoking Booklet
Call:	1-800-LUNG-USA (800-586-4872)
Mail To:	American Lung Association P.O. Box 596-FB Pamphlet #0022 New York, NY 10116-0596

Health Information
REYE'S SYNDROME

☆ As a teacher you spend more time with children than just about anyone, so you should know about the diseases that can affect them. This free **informational packet on Reye's Syndrome**—a disease that can affect the liver and brain of children from infancy to 19 years of age—provides you with important information. Learn more about this currently incurable ailment and the work being done by the National Reye's Syndrome Research Foundation to find a cure.

Call: 1-800-233-7393
Ask For: Information Packet on Reye's Syndrome

Diabetes Information
TELEPHONE DIRECTORY

☆ Diabetes is not a rare condition. It actually afflicts about 14 million Americans. You should have updated information in the event one of your students is diabetic. An easy way to get the information is to send for your **free Tele-Library card** which helps you access a service by LifeScan that provides prerecorded information 24 hours a day on a variety of diabetes topics.

Send: A long SASE
Ask For: LifeScan Tele-Library Card
Mail To: LifeScan Tele-Library Card
485 Madison Ave.
4th Floor
New York, NY 10022

Frugal Times Sample Issue

ON THE CHEAP

☆ Master the art of saving money when you order a **free sample issue of *Frugal Times*,** the helpful newsletter that's packed with money-saving ideas. The theme of this publication is "Making-Do With Dignity," and it helps you accomplish that by telling you how to save on everything from food to utility bills.

Send: A long SASE with two first-class stamps

Ask For: Sample Issue of *Frugal Times*

Mail To: Frugal Times
12534 Valley View, #234F
Garden Grove, CA 92645

Healthy Diet Help

READ THE LABEL

☆ There's one sure way to know if you're eating the right foods and getting the nutritional value you need to stay healthy by avoiding too much sugar, calories, or fat. **"Labeling Logic"** is a free brochure that tells you how to wade your way through the new food labels and make important diet determinations. With detailed write-ups and helpful graphics, this takes the mystery out of the label laws.

Send: A long SASE

Ask For: ADA Labeling Logic Brochure

Mail To: Labeling Logic Brochure
ADA National Center for Nutrition and Dietetics
P.O. Box 39101
Chicago, IL 60639

Household Hints

SALT SAVERS

☆ You may think that salt is just used to add a little flavor to your favorite dishes. But did you know that you can use it to make Christmas decorations, take out stains, or make craft projects? Send for these **free brochures from Morton Salt** and you'll learn all about things you can do with salt that you probably never knew before.

Send: Your name & address

Ask For: Morton Salt Household Hints/Arts & Crafts Brochures

Mail To: Morton Salt
Dept. FR
100 N. Riverside Plaza
Chicago, IL 60606

Ruler

HISTORY RULES

☆ You can measure up a bit of history with this ruler that features the **American Flags and the Presidents of the United States.** One side is decorated with American flags from the earliest Navy Jack to the 50-star variety. The back side of the ruler has pictures and dates of office for each President from George Washington to Bill Clinton.

Send: $1.00 P&H

Ask For: Flag/Presidents Ruler

Mail To: Esther's E-Z Shop
Dept. PFR
P.O. Box 1831
Pomona, CA 91769

Historic Event Postcards

FRONT-PAGE POSTCARDS

☆ Here's an item that makes a great addition to the bulletin board or a nice way to send a greeting to a friend. **Space History Front-Page Postcards and Civil War Front-Page Postcards** are standard-sized postcards with a recreation of newspaper coverage of great American events. The space set features everything from the shuttle to spacewalks, while the Civil War set covers Fort Sumter to Bull Run. Order one or both.

Send: $1.60 P&H for each set

Ask For: Space History Postcards and/or Civil War Events Postcards

Mail To: Esther's E-Z Shop
Dept. PC
P.O. Box 1831
Pomona, CA 91769

Eraser Set

MAKE NO MISTAKE

☆ Mistakes are inevitable, especially with young students. That's a good reason to have this set of six 1½" **sea animal erasers** on hand. They come in a variety of seagoing styles and make good prizes for classroom projects.

Send: $1.65 P&H

Ask For: Sea Eraser Set

Mail To: Marlene Monroe
Dept. SAE
6210 Ridge Manor Dr.
Memphis, TN 38115

Storybooks

CLASSIC TALES

☆ If you like reading to your class of younger students, then you should introduce them to the classics. We don't mean *War and Peace*. But how about *Snow White and the Seven Dwarfs*, *Aladdin and the Magic Lamp*, or *The Jungle Book?* Send off for this **set of two Original Enchanted Tales.** Complete with cheerful illustrations, these are lively retellings of the stories you grew up with and the ones today's kids will enjoy.

Send: $2.00 P&H for two

Ask For: Original Enchanted Tales FB Offer/LF1-12 Series (suppliers' choice)

Mail To: Jaye Products
Books & Crafts
P.O. Box 61471
Fort Myers, FL 33906-1471

Teddy Bear Ornament

A TEDDY BEAR CHRISTMAS

☆ If you plan to have a tree in your classroom for Christmas, or if you're looking for a nice ornament to hang on your tree at home, order this delightful **Teddy Bear Ornament.** Framed in a traditional bell cutout, this colorful teddy bear sits holding a green, white, and red ball and is approximately 3" in height.

Send: $1.75 P&H for one; $2.90 for two

Ask For: Teddy Bear Christmas Ornament

Mail To: Nutri-Art
6437 Massey Estates Cove
Memphis, TN 38119

Nutritional Teaching Aids

IT'S IN THE CARDS

☆ You want to get the point across to your class about good nutrition, but your students keep dozing off during those long lectures. Make learning fun with a variety of **games and teaching aids** that all drive home the point about learning how to eat right. Send for this **free brochure** that tells you how to get card games, coloring books, and puzzles that all deal with healthy eating.

Send: A long SASE

Ask For: Nutritional Teaching Aid Brochure

Mail To: Nutri-Art
6437 Massey Estates Cove
Memphis, TN 38119

Address Tag Key Chains

TWO-IN-ONE

☆ Here's an item that either makes a great classroom prize or keep it for yourself to make sure your bags never get lost. This set of **colorful plastic address tags and key chains** work either way. The set comes with a double key ring and has a tag with an insert for writing down names and addresses and can be attached to camera straps, briefcases, or school totes.

Send: $1.30 P&H for four; $2 for eight

Ask For: Plastic Name Tag Set

Mail To: Marlene Monroe
Dept. TAGS
6210 Ridge Manor Dr.
Memphis, TN 38115

Crafting Dough

DOUGH-SEE-DOUGH

☆ Your imagination is the limit on creativity when you send for this **¼ lb. packet of Rainbow Scented Crafting Dough™.** The dough comes in eight different brilliant colors, each having a unique aroma. The supplier will pick from orange, lemon, strawberry, tropical punch, mint, rootbeer, raspberry, or cinnamon. It's safe for kids of all ages, and it's nontoxic. Use it to build motor skills as well as imagination. Your crafting dough also comes with a free 10-page activity booklet packed with fun ideas.

Send: $1.50

Ask For: Rainbow Scented Dough (suppliers' choice on aromas)

Mail To: ABC, Inc.
2070 Oak Grove Blvd.
Milwaukee, OR 97267

White House Tour Book

PRESIDENTIAL ADDRESS

☆ Don't despair if you can't take your class to Washington, DC, to visit The White House. Let The White House come to you with the **free White House Photo Tour Book.** This 32-page, glossy, full-color book takes you on a tour through every room in The White House—from the Oval Office to the Rose Garden. No room is off limits to you and your class with this book. (Please allow at least 12 weeks for delivery.)

Send: Your name & address

Ask For: White House Photo Tour Book

Mail To: The White House
Washington, DC 20500

Additional Resources

The following organizations can provide help to kids and families or might be able to provide materials on a variety of topics you can use in the classroom.

Adam Walsh Child Resource Center
319 Clematis St., Ste. 409
West Palm Beach, FL 33401

American Association for Protecting Children
c/o American Humane Association
63 Inverness Dr. East
Englewood, CO 80112

A Wish with Wings
P.O. Box 3457
Arlington, TX 76010

Big Brothers/Big Sisters of America
230 N. 13th St.
Philadelphia, PA 19107

Boy Scouts of America
1325 W. Walnut Hill Lane
P.O. Box 152079
Irving, TX 75015-2079

Camp Fire Girls
4601 Madison Ave.
Kansas City, MO 64112

Child Abuse Listening and Mediation (CALM)
P.O. Box 90754
Santa Barbara, CA 93190-0754

Child Find of America
P.O. Box 277
New Paltz, NY 12561

Childhelp U.S.A., Inc.
6463 Independence Ave.
Woodland Hills, CA 91370

Children's Aid International
6270 Melrose Ave.
P.O. Box 480155
Los Angeles, CA 90048

Children's Defense Fund
122 C St. NW, St. 400
Washington, DC 20001

Children's Rights of America
655 Ulmerton Rd., Ste. 4A
Largo, FL 34641

Child Welfare League of America
440 First St., NW, Ste. 310
Washington, DC 20001

Compassion International
3955 Cragwood Dr.
P.O. Box 7000
Colorado Springs, CO 80993

Find the Children
11811 W. Olympic Blvd.
Los Angeles, CA 90064

Foster Parents Plan
155 Plan Way, Dept. K024
Warwick, RI 02886

Girl Scouts of the USA
830 Third Ave.
New York, NY 10022

Make-A-Wish Foundation of America
2600 N. Central Ave., Ste. 936
Phoenix, AZ 85004

Missing Children Help Center
410 Ware Blvd., Ste. 400
Tampa, FL 33619

National Committee for Prevention of
Child Abuse
332 S. Michigan Ave., Ste. 1600
Chicago, IL 60604-4357

National Exchange Club Foundation for the
Prevention of Child Abuse
3050 Central Ave.
Toledo, OH 43606

National Federation of Parents for
Drug-Free Youth
P.O. Box 3878
St. Louis, MO 65802

National PTA
700 N. Rush St.
Chicago, IL 60611

Parents Anonymous
6733 S. Sepulveda, Ste. 270
Los Angeles, CA 90045

Parents Helping Parents
535 Race St., Ste. 220
San Jose, CA 95126

The Runaway and Homeless Youth Shelters
Department of Health & Human Services
Office of Human Development Services
Washington, DC 20201-0001

Save the Children Federation
54 Wilton Rd., Box 921
Westport, CT 06681

Stepfamily Association of America, Inc.
215 Centennial Mall South, Ste. 212
Lincoln, NE 68508-1834

Sunshine Foundation
4010 Levick St.
Philadelphia, PA 19135

Toughlove International
P.O. Box 1069
Doylestown, PA 18901

FREE   FREE   FREE

Something for nothing!!! Hundreds of dollars' worth of items in each issue of **FREEBIES MAGAZINE.** Five times a year (for over 14 years), each issue features at least 100 FREE and low-postage-&-handling-only offers. Useful, informative, and fun items. Household information, catalogs, recipes, health/medical information, toys for kids, samples of everything from tea bags to jewelry—every offer of every issue is yours for FREE, or for a small postage and handling charge!

Have you purchased a "Free Things" book before—only to find that the items were unavailable? That won't happen with FREEBIES—all of our offers are authenticated (and verified for accuracy) with the suppliers!

❒ YES – Send me 5 issues for only $4.95
(save $4.00 off the regular subscription rate!)

❒ YES – I want to save even more. Send me 10 issues for only $7.95 (save 70% off the cover price!)

❒ Payment Enclosed, or Charge my   ❒ VISA   ❒ MasterCard

Card Number ⎯ ⎯ ⎯ ⎯   ⎯ ⎯ ⎯ ⎯   ⎯ ⎯ ⎯ ⎯   ⎯ ⎯ ⎯ ⎯   Exp. Date ⎯ ⎯ ⎯ ⎯

Name _____ | Daytime Phone#
Address _____ | (   ) _____
City _____ State _____ Zip _____ | (in case we have a question about your subscription)

SEND TO: FREEBIES MAGAZINE/Teacher Offer
1135 Eugenia Place, Carpinteria, CA 93013